A MAGICAL PLACE

TORONTO ISLAND AND ITS PEOPLE

Bill Freeman

Contemporary photography by David Laurence

JAMES LORIMER & COMPANY LTD., PUBLISHERS

TORONTO

James Lorimer & Company Ltd. acknowledges the support of the Department of Canadian Heritage and the Ontario Arts Council in the development of writing and publishing in Canada. We acknowledge the support of the Canada Council for the Arts for our publishing program.

Canadä

Canadian Cataloguing in Publication Data

Freeman, Bill, 1938-
A magical place: Toronto Island and its people
Includes index.
ISBN 1-55028-670-6
1. Toronto Islands (Ont.) -- History. 2. Toronto Islands (Ont.) -- Pictorial works I. Title.
FC3097.52.F73 1999   971.3'541   C99-931822-5
F1059.5.T686T67 1999

James Lorimer & Company Ltd., Publishers
35 Britain Street
Toronto, Ontario
M5A 1R7
Printed and bound in Canada.

For Islanders all: past, present and future, but especially Paulette, who, like the Island, has enriched my life.

PHOTO CREDITS

CONTENTS

ACKNOWLEDGEMENTS

My first confession is that I am an Islander. This book would never have been written if it were not for the fact that over the years that I have lived on Toronto Island I have come to appreciate its history and the people who created this very special world.

For me the book has been a chance to enrich my understanding of my own community. The detailed research has given me the opportunity to reach back into the Island's past and discover scores of half-forgotten characters and events that still inform the consciousness of Islanders like the figures or events of mythology.

My first acknowledgement, then, is to Islanders themselves. They are the ones who created their own history

and shared that history with me. Some of them include Liz Amer, Peter Newman, David Harris, Brent Rutherford, Mary Hay, Madeleine McLaughlin, Jerry and Leida Englar, Peter Holt, Sarah Miller, Kay Walker, Peter and Enid Cridland, Lorraine Filyer and Morris Hill. Thanks all.

One person deserves special mention. Albert Fulton, the Island archivist, has amassed a remarkable collection of both written and visual material on Toronto Island. In his generous manner Albert shared this material with me as well as his knowledge and insights about the Island.

Other archivists and librarians were helpful both in tracking down elusive details for the text and collecting old photos. These include staff at both the Metropolitan Toronto Reference Library and the City of Toronto Archives.

The text is only part of a book such as this. The other vital ingredient is the visuals and particularly the contemporary photos. Watching the careful, thoughtful way that David Laurence went about setting up each shot has given me increased respect for the art of photography. The handsome photos on these pages are a testament to the creativity of his work.

Finally, I would like to thank the people at James Lorimer & Company Ltd., Publishers. Diane Young shepherded this book through the publishing house, giving scores of helpful suggestions. Jim Lorimer was never very far from this project. He originally conceived the idea of doing a book on the Island as part of a series on Toronto neighbourhoods, and he established the format of a generous mix of text and illustrations that I believe has resulted in a satisfying book.

Bill Freeman

Map

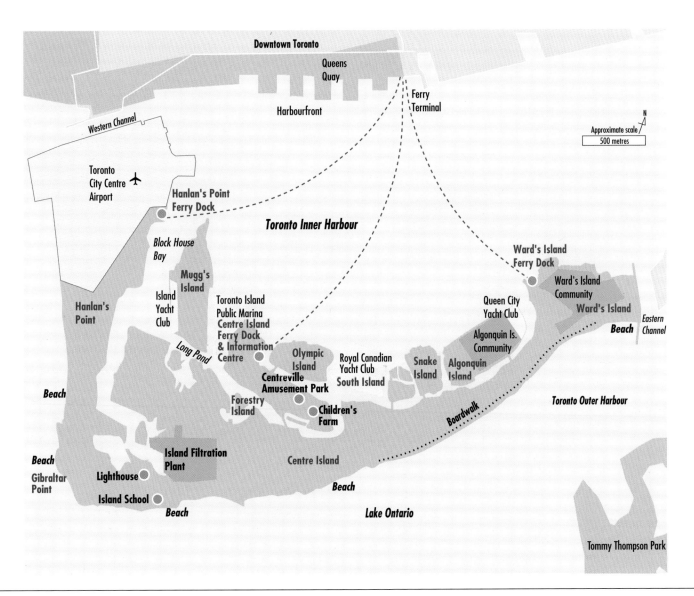

INTRODUCTION

The Queen City Yacht Club, Algonquin Island

In the imaginations of many, Toronto Island is a magical place, uniquely different from any other neighbourhood in the city. During the fifteen-minute ferryboat ride across the harbour, the visitor is transported from the stark, concrete and glass towers of the downtown, with its traffic and press of people, to the soft, low-lying, crescent-shaped island where there are no cars and even the houses have a more natural, human scale.

As the boat churns across the bay, the Toronto skyline recedes and the Island comes more sharply into view. The

Boating in Centre Island lagoon

land appears as a low-lying ribbon of green rising out of the blue of the water, touched by a big expanse of sky. The

closer the boat gets the greater the features take on definition. Trees take shape along with acres of grass, inlets, boats and buildings. Slowly the dock comes into view and with a roar of the reversing propeller, the ferry arrives.

Once on the Island there is much to explore. The park, with 820 acres, has everything from beaches and lagoons to picnic areas and amusement rides. There are islands that can only be visited by boat and isolated reserves for nesting

Amusement Park, Centre Island

birds. The 262 houses in the community, which occupy about forty acres on Ward's and Algonquin Islands, were mostly built as cottages. They are small and over the years residents have fashioned them into eccentric styles to meet their needs. There are bicycles everywhere, people are on

Beach, Centre Island

Ferry docks, Centre Island

the street walking and children run free in the full confidence that this is a safe place to live.

But despite the idyllic setting there are few communities that have experienced as much conflict as Toronto Island. Over the years there have been competing visions that have shaped its complex and colourful history. Some people have believed that the Island should be a place dedicated solely to the use of the public, and any private use of the land was deemed to be incompatible with public use of the park. The other vision was that the community enhanced the public's enjoyment of the Island and was not incompatible with public use. The compromise that was finally reached between these two visions saved the Island community and provided a unique urban park that is enjoyed by well over a million visitors each year.

This book is a celebration of that compromise, but it goes much beyond that to reveal the legends and history of this magical place. In fact, the story of the Island begins at that moment where legend and history merge.

2 Third Street, Ward's Island

THE GOVERNOR AND ISLAND DEFENCES

The Island is one of the prominent features of the north shore of Lake Ontario and has shaped the life, industry and commerce of the area since long before recorded history. Even the name "Toronto" is thought to come from the Island. In the language of the Mississauga Indians, who occupied the western part of Lake Ontario when Europeans arrived, the word Toronto means "trees standing in the water," a normal occurrence on the Island, then and now. Not only this, the Island provided the chief geographical feature that led to the establishment of the city: a safe and defensible harbour.

The Island is a long sandbar formed by material

York harbour, looking west from the Don River, 1793, from a watercolour by Elizabeth Simcoe

eroded from the Scarborough Bluffs. When the French traders came along the north shore of Lake Ontario in the seventeenth century, travelling from the east by canoe with their native guides, they found a six-kilometre-long peninsula that was half a kilometre wide. At the base of the peninsula, where the Eastern Gap is today, was a "carrying place," where travellers portaged from the lake into the quiet waters of Toronto Bay.

This is a description of the Island and the bay by Joseph Bouchette, an early European traveller:

John Graves Simcoe, 1791, from a portrait by Jean Laurent Mosnier

> *I still distinctly recollect the untamed aspect which the country exhibited when first I entered the beautiful basin... Dense and trackless forests lined the margin of the lake, and reflected their inverted images in its glassy surface. The wandering savage had constructed his ephemeral habitation beneath their luxuriant foliage—the group then consisting of two families of Mississaugas—and the bay and neighbouring marshes were the hitherto uninvaded haunts of immense coveys of wild fowl: indeed they were so abundant as in some measure to annoy us during the night.*

In the folklore of the Mississauga Indians the peninsula was a place with medicinal benefits. Often they camped on its shores and fished in the bay for salmon, whitefish, pickerel, bass, sturgeon and other fish.

The first Europeans who came into the area were French fur traders who established a trading post near the mouth of the Humber River. It was a good location. Native groups could travel by canoe along the lake, and there was a route up the Humber that led to Lake Simcoe, Georgian Bay and the

York harbour, looking east from Bathurst Street, 1793, after a drawing by Elizabeth Simcoe

north. For many years the trading post turned a healthy profit.

But it was politics, more than economics, that led to the establishment of the city. The British threatened the French in North America for supremacy, and in 1758 they captured forts on Lake Ontario. On July 28 of that year the French commander burned his post at Toronto and retreated with fifteen soldiers to Montreal. Finally, with the Battle of the Plains of Abraham at Quebec in September 1759, the struggle ended in British domination.

For thirty years little happened along the north shore of Lake Ontario, but then politics once again determined the history of the area. After the American Revolutionary War was over in 1784, some 20,000 United Empire Loyalists came to settle in Upper Canada, which came to be known as Ontario. The British sent Colonel John Graves Simcoe to be lieutenant governor of the colony in 1791 and he stayed until 1799. Simcoe was very concerned that the capital of Upper Canada, located at Niagara-on-the-Lake (then called Newark), was indefensible because it was just across the river from the United States. He was determined to find a capital away from the border that could be more easily defended.

The lieutenant governor considered various locations and finally settled on Toronto. There were a number of reasons for his choice. In those days the most common form of travel in the colony was by water. This meant that the capital had to be on the lake, it needed to have a good harbour and above all, the harbour had to have natural defences. Toronto, with its long peninsula protecting the harbour, provided the perfect location.

On the evening of July 29, 1793, Simcoe, along with his wife, Elizabeth, their two smallest children, and various aides and members of the military, set out across the lake to the newly chosen capital. The lieutenant governor had already visited Toronto, and men from the Queen's Rangers Regiment were hard at work clearing the forest, setting up camp and laying out the town, which Simcoe renamed York.

The lieutenant governor had great enthusiasm for the site. He described it as "the best harbour on the Lakes," but he was most excited because he felt the harbour could be strongly fortified. He wrote:

I found it to be without comparison the most proper situation for an arsenal in every extent of that word that can be met with in this province. The spit of sand, which forms its entrance, is capable of being so fortified with a few heavy guns as to prevent any vessel from entering the harbour or from remaining within it.

Simcoe called the western tip of the peninsula "Gibraltar Point," not because it looked like the rocky fortress that guards the entrance to the Mediterranean, but because he planned to build an impregnable battery on the point that would guard the harbour's entrance. In 1794, work was begun on two defensible storehouses and a guardhouse.

Elizabeth Simcoe, the lieutenant governor's wife, was equally enthusiastic about their new home. She was a remarkable woman: an artist, naturalist and diarist. A few days after the voyage across the lake she visited the peninsula for the first time.

We crossed the bay opposite the camp and rode by the lake side to the end of the peninsula. We met with some good natural meadows and several ponds. The trees are mostly of the poplar kind covered with wild vines and there are some fir. On the ground were everlasting peas creeping in abundance, of a purple colour. I am told they are good to eat when boiled and some pretty white flowers like lily of the valley.

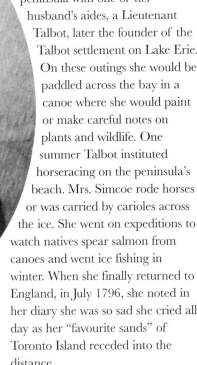

Elizabeth Simcoe, 1790, from a watercolour by Mary Anne Burges

Over the next three years Mrs. Simcoe frequently went to the peninsula with one of her husband's aides, a Lieutenant Talbot, later the founder of the Talbot settlement on Lake Erie. On these outings she would be paddled across the bay in a canoe where she would paint or make careful notes on plants and wildlife. One summer Talbot instituted horseracing on the peninsula's beach. Mrs. Simcoe rode horses or was carried by carioles across the ice. She went on expeditions to watch natives spear salmon from canoes and went ice fishing in winter. When she finally returned to England, in July 1796, she noted in her diary she was so sad she cried all day as her "favourite sands" of Toronto Island receded into the distance.

Lieutenant Governor Simcoe had accomplished a great deal in his short stay in the colony. However, he proved to be wrong on what he thought was the site's most important advantage: its natural defences. When the Americans invaded in April 1813 they landed their troops in Humber Bay, at what is now called Sunnyside Beach, well out of the range of the British guns. With superior numbers and arms, they quickly took Fort York and occupied the town. Fortunately for the occupants, they stayed only a week, but before they left they demolished the blockhouse at Gibraltar Point.

THE LIGHTHOUSE

In the first half of the nineteenth century most people arrived at the town of York by water. (The name was changed back to Toronto in 1834.) The government of the day recognized that it was essential that the harbour be well marked, and in 1803 the legislature approved the building of a lighthouse on the peninsula at the point of land where the long sandbar takes an almost ninety-degree turn to the north. This has come to be called Gibraltar Point, on what is today called Centre Island, although it is some distance from the place where Simcoe built the battery.

The lighthouse was built out of grey limestone brought across the lake from Queenston. The structure is hexagonal in shape, and at its base the stones are six-feet thick. Originally the lighthouse rose seventy-feet high, and in 1832 another twelve feet were added to bring its total height to eighty-two feet. For 150 years, from 1808 to 1958, a powerful lamp, fuelled first by sperm whale oil then coal oil, and finally electricity, burned from the lighthouse. For many years it was the first sign of Toronto that travellers arriving by water spotted, and as they left, it was the last point of reference before it sunk beneath the horizon.

At the same time the lighthouse was erected, a small

Lighthouse, Centre Island, circa 1817, from a watercolour by Willliam Armstrong

house was built close to it, and J.P. Rademuller, the lighthouse keeper, became the first permanent Island resident. He met a terrible end. Legend has it that Rademuller was involved in the illegal liquor trade. One night in January 1815 he was visited by soldiers from the garrison at Fort York. When they became too drunk the lighthouse keeper refused them more liquor. They became enraged, turned on him and beat him to death.

Two of the soldiers were brought to trial, but acquitted for lack of evidence because the body could not be found. Years later, in fact, a skeleton was found on the Island which was felt to be that of the unfortunate lighthouse keeper. But some believe that the keeper has never really left the lighthouse. Hollow thuds and thumping sounds, coming from the bleak tower in the middle of the night, suggest that the ghost of Rademuller continues to haunt the lonely place to this very day.

The rather grim old pillar remains at Gibraltar Point. When it was built it was twenty-five feet from the water's edge. Today it is at least four times that distance from the shore as the sands of the Island have continued to shift with the water currents. The lighthouse is the oldest building in Toronto and Canada's oldest standing lighthouse.

THE DUEL FOR HONOUR

Before dawn on the morning of April 3, 1812, Dr. William Baldwin rose out of his bed, dressed and slipped out of his house. Baldwin, a lawyer, doctor, architect and political reformer, had been insulted by John Macdonnell, a Tory and the newly appointed attorney general of the colony, with "expressions so wanton and ungentlemanly" that Baldwin demanded an apology. When an apology was refused, Baldwin demanded satisfaction. The challenge was taken up by Macdonnell, and a pistol duel on the peninsula was arranged by their seconds.

That fateful morning Baldwin met with his second, Lieutenant Thomas Taylor, and the two men walked east across the bridge over the Don River, pausing briefly while Baldwin wrote out his will. Then they continued along the path toward the peninsula. As they walked they could see Macdonnell and his second, Duncan Cameron, crossing the bay by sleigh.

As the sun rose at six a.m. the combatants met at a lonely spot on the peninsula. They selected their pistols and were placed back to back. They paced off the distance, and the signal to fire was given.

Macdonnell stood with his arms at his side. Baldwin levelled his gun, paused and then aimed away, discharging his pistol harmlessly into the bushes. The duel was over, and although both men lived, their honour had been satisfied.

Six months later John Macdonnell lay dead on the battlefield at Queenston Heights. Dr. William Baldwin went on to become an important political figure in Upper Canada as both a reformer and advocate of "responsible government." His more famous son, Robert Baldwin, was a major political leader in the 1840s and helped to form the first responsible government in Canada in 1848 with Louis LaFontaine.

William Baldwin, circa 1850, from a painting by Theophile Hamel

TRULY AN ISLAND

It was not long after the town was established that the peninsula's resources began to be exploited. Muddy York, as the town was sometimes called, developed rapidly. From a population of 703 people in 1812, it grew to 1,719 in 1826 and by 1834 had exceeded 9,000. By the 1830s it was the largest centre in Upper Canada.

Sanitary conditions in the town were in such a primitive state that the once crystal clear waters of the harbour soon became murky and polluted. But still the peninsula and the harbour remained the chief places of recreation for the population largely because it was too difficult to travel anywhere else.

The first hotel, called "The Retreat on the Peninsula," was opened in 1833 by Michael O'Connor, a veteran of the Napoleonic Wars, near the narrow neck of land that attached the peninsula to the mainland, about where the Eastern Gap is today.

Privat's hotel, where the Eastern Gap is today, circa 1850, from a watercolour by Owen Staples

O'Connor was somewhat of an innovator as well as an entrepreneur. He was the first to establish a regular boat connection with the town by running a horse ferry from the foot of Church Street to his wharf. The hotel was never very successful, perhaps because it developed a reputation as a rowdy place of heavy gambling and drinking.

Unfortunately for O'Connor, two years after he established his hotel it failed, but soon there were new proprietors. Rechristened the Peninsula Hotel the new operators, Messrs. Anderton and Palin, placed ads on New Year's Day 1835 promising "a pleasant and healthy retreat for individuals and families desirous of changing the air of the City for the salubrious atmosphere of the Island."

Storms were always a problem on the exposed peninsula. When the winds blew from the southeast the waves built up across the whole reach of Lake Ontario and pounded onto the beach. On the night of April 13, 1858, John Quinn and his family, who had recently bought the Peninsula Hotel, were preparing for a party when a furious storm rose. Quinn's daughter, Jenny, gave this description of events:

We found mother balancing on a board in the churning water with my baby brother in her arms and my sister Elizabeth clinging precariously to her skirts. She seemed to be standing on the only timber left from the hotel, which was disintegrating and shortly disappeared.

Quinn managed to save his family, but by the next morning the hotel had completely washed away. The storm had cut a channel through the isthmus four to five feet deep and 200 feet wide. The peninsula was now truly an island, and Toronto Harbour had two entrances: the Western and Eastern Gaps.

THE HARBOUR

In the first half of the nineteenth century much of Toronto life centred around the harbour and the Island. (Curiously, the peninsula was often called "the Island" even before the storm of 1858.) It was a port town. Eventually, schooners took over from square-riggers and then an increasing number of steamboats plied the lake. These large side- and stern-wheelers provided comfortable connections to such centres as Kingston, Cobourg, Port Hope, Hamilton, the Niagara Peninsula ports, Rochester and Oswego.

York from Gibralter Point, 1828, from a drawing by James Gray, aquatinted by Joshua Gleadah

By 1828 a waterway connecting Lake Ontario and the Hudson River via Oswego and the Erie Canal was opened. In 1848 the Welland Canal gave shipping entrance to the upper lakes, and the canal system down the St. Lawrence provided water access to Montreal, the Atlantic and beyond. By the 1830s wharves proliferated along the waterfront along with warehouses and taverns frequented by dockworkers.

The harbour was the centre of commercial life for the city, but it was also used year-round for recreation. In summer, residents sailed on the protected waters of the bay or rowed small skiffs out to the Island for picnics on the long sand beach and protected lagoons. In winter, there was iceboating, sleighing, skating and curling on the harbour. In those days there was a balance between commercial and recreational uses of the harbour, and the role of Toronto as a major port seemed assured.

Then, in the 1850s, the railway age suddenly arrived. In 1851 construction began on the Northern Railway to Georgian Bay. By 1855 the Great Western Railway was extended from Hamilton to Toronto, and in 1856 the Grand Trunk Railway linked Toronto and Montreal and was extended westward to Windsor and beyond by 1859.

The railways ushered in a new industrial age. Soon the majority of goods and passengers were arriving in the city by rail. Shipping as a means of transportation was in

The Queen's Wharf at the foot of Bathurst Street, circa 1910

decline. The railway tracks were built along the Esplanade, separating the city from its harbour.

By the 1860s large factories were being constructed along the waterfront where the two transportation systems met. Thousands of workers streamed into the area every day to labour in the factories or load and unload trains and ships. By 1871 the city had a population of 56,092 and by 1891 it had grown to a phenomenal 181,216, despite the worldwide depression suffered during those twenty years.

Through the entire nineteenth century the harbour and wharves were in private hands. In the 1870s the Eastern Gap was dredged so that it became the main harbour entrance, but it had to be dredged on a regular basis to keep the channel navigable. No one was willing to take on the costs of dredging and ensuring that the wharves were in good repair. Finally, in 1911 the Toronto Harbour Commission (THC) was created by the federal government to manage the harbour in the public interest.

Not long after it was established, the THC undertook a massive redevelopment project that completely transformed the waterfront. Thousands of acres of land were created by filling in the water between the railroad tracks and what is

City of Toronto *steamer, circa 1915, from a drawing by Charles Snider*

today Queen's Quay. The huge marsh in Ashbridge's Bay was also filled to create additional land. Much of this new property soon became devoted to industrial and warehousing uses and new wharves were created.

From the time that this work was completed in the 1920s until today, there has been another transformation along the waterfront. The port as an entrance for cargo and passengers into the city has continued to decline. Today the main port facility is limited to one hundred acres on the Eastern Gap, at the foot of Cherry Street.

Indeed, by the 1960s the harbour's commercial uses had declined so much that it was primarily used for recreation. Since then thousands of acres of land adjacent to the harbour along Queen's Quay has been redeveloped for residential, commercial, recreational and cultural uses. Today the waterfront is the fastest-growing neighbourhood in the City of Toronto. There are 5,000 apartment and condominium units, and another 17,000 units are in the planning stages.

Toronto bay, 1886, from a painting by George Reid

Toronto Harbour today

Boat Tours on Toronto Bay and the Blue Beyond

Steamboat service around Lake Ontario did not collapse with the coming of the railroads, but it changed substantially. In the latter part of the nineteenth century, as the city and the surrounding area grew rapidly in population, the area also grew in wealth. The middle and upper classes had money to spend on holidays and weekend getaways. It did not happen overnight, but the steamboats that plied the lake slowly changed from an essential means of transportation into tour boats.

Toronto was the centre of this new industry on Lake Ontario. As early as 1855 "moonlight tours" were offered on Toronto Bay. By the 1860s trips across to the Niagara Peninsula to visit the falls were very popular, and by the 1890s two-day tours through the Thousand Islands, with elaborate meals and dancing, attracted many tourists on summer weekends. Canadians were part of this growing tourist trade, but Americans increasingly came to enjoy these exotic lake cruises that would take them to foreign ports such as Toronto.

The height of the era of big tour boats was in the period prior to the First World War, but services continued right through to the 1940s. A number of ships were commissioned for this trade. The *Cayuga*, for example, was built in 1906

Cayuga, *Eastern Gap, 1918, from a photograph by Charles Williams*

Noronic, *1930, from a photograph by William James*

A tour boat, Centre Island lagoon

and remained in service until 1957. It was estimated that she carried over fifteen million passengers in the course of her service.

After the Second World War the lifestyle of Canadians changed and the tour boat industry declined. Families bought cars and spent their holidays at summer cottages or travelling abroad. Another reason for the decline was the burning of the largest and best-appointed passenger vessel on the Great Lakes, the 385-foot *Noronic*.

The *Noronic* was built in 1913, and in her years of service she carried millions of passengers. On September 17, 1949, the boat was tied up in Toronto Harbour, close to the foot of Yonge Street, when she caught fire at one o'clock in the morning. In fifteen minutes the fire had spread from stem to stern. Some passengers managed to throw themselves overboard to escape the flames, but 119 people lost their lives in the raging inferno, all but one were American citizens. This tragedy sent shock waves through the industry in Canada, and it never fully recovered.

However, in the last few years, a new tour boat industry has been created that rivals the passenger industry of old. Today over twenty-five boats offer a wide range of tours out of Toronto Harbour. Many are one-hour excursions around the bay, others offer tours through the Island's lagoons and still others go out into Lake Ontario to circumnavigate the Island. There are glass-roofed tour boats that can carry sixty passengers, tall ships that cruise the harbour under sail and moonlight party tours that feature dancing, and can carry up to 600 people. There are now even boats that connect across the lake to Niagara Peninsula ports.

The key to this revival, according to Kathie Rogers, president of one of the tour boat companies, is: "The people of Toronto are finally discovering what tourists have known for decades—that this city has one of the most exciting and enjoyable waterfronts in North America."

SAILING THE BLUE WATERS

Recreational boating has long been a popular activity for many Torontonians. Today sailboats and powerboats of all sizes cruise the bay and the lake; people in canoes and row boats meander through the complex of lagoons on the Island, and there are a number of clubs, both on and off the Island, that provide services to boaters and teach people to sail, row or canoe.

The origins of yachting in the city go back to the earliest days of settlement. In 1850 a group of prominent sailors met to discuss establishing a club to encourage sailing. By 1852 they had formed themselves into the Toronto Yacht Club, and in 1854, with the consent of Queen Victoria, they took on the name of Royal Canadian Yacht Club, the RCYC.

Initially the RCYC clubhouse was housed in various boats moored along the waterfront, but in 1869-70 they built their first clubhouse on the Esplanade at the foot of Simcoe Street in the city. The members were never very

Royal Canadian Yacht Club

happy with this location. The railway yards were adjacent to their property, and with all of the shunting of the trains, and the encroaching industrial life of the growing city, it was not very conducive to the gentle art of sailing.

Consequently, in 1880 the club selected ten acres of land on the bay side of the Island overlooking the city. They sold their esplanade property to the railroad for a tidy profit, began to improve the Island property and build their new clubhouse. In June of 1881 they moved into their handsome new clubhouse, which had a large veranda and a tower for viewing races, with reading, drawing, billiard and dining rooms furnished in pine.

Queen City Yacht Club

The move of the RCYC contributed a great deal to the Island's development. Soon there was a lively social scene during the summers at the Island clubhouse. Prominent families of the business and political elite played an important role in the life of the club. Membership grew, with over sixty yachts flying the club burgee by the 1880s. Club members were active in the racing scene around Lake Ontario and beyond. Women, who were excluded from the activities of most clubs in this period, even began to play a part when Wednesdays became "Ladies' Days."

In 1904 the RCYC clubhouse burned to the ground, but by the next season a new larger clubhouse had been built. In 1918, the last year of the First World War, this building also burned. It was 1922 before a new clubhouse was rebuilt and opened. It is this building that is in use today.

The RCYC island clubhouse is one of the most impressive buildings in the city, and the site, overlooking the harbour and the city, adds to its sense of grandeur. The large white wooden structure is fronted with two-story-high pillars that enclose a double veranda on both the first and second floors. On the ground floor is an elegant dining room, trophy room and a variety of other facilities for club members. On the second floor is an immense ballroom decorated in the style of a ship's saloon. At either end of the ballroom are murals by Owen Staples, a well-known Toronto painter.

Sailing is the central activity of the RCYC. Boats of various sizes are moored along the lagoons. Sheds house the dinghy fleet and a section has been set aside for the Junior Club, where an active sailing school operates every summer. But there are other activities such as swimming, tennis and croquet. The large green in the front of the clubhouse is set aside for lawn bowling, and on most hot summer days men and women dressed in white can be found having a leisurely game.

Other yacht clubs have also found a home on Toronto Island. The Queen City Yacht Club (QCYC) was first founded in 1889. For the first thirty years the QCYC had clubhouses on the city side of the harbour, but with the threat of redevelopment along the waterfront in 1920 the club members decided to relocate to Toronto Island. By the next year the QCYC had their new clubhouse built on Sunfish Island (today called Algonquin Island) overlooking both the Ward's lagoon and the harbour. This clubhouse is still in use today and is the centre of an active sailing and social life.

The Island Yacht Club, with its clubhouse and mooring on Mugg's Island, was founded as recently as 1950. Jewish people found that they were not able to get memberships in the two other clubs and were determined to establish their own facilities. Since that time it has become a very active club with many well-known sailors.

There are other boating facilities on Toronto Island. The Marina, on Centre Island, is a private facility where boats can be moored, and a number of small clubs are located there.

TORONTO ICEBOATS

Sailing in Toronto Bay is a summer activity, but in winter there is another sailing sport that has long been of interest to people in the city: iceboating, the fastest, non-mechanized sport in the world. It is not for the faint of heart.

Until recent decades, Toronto Bay would freeze solid for six or eight weeks every winter. Ice can form or disappear remarkably quickly, and iceboaters have to be ready on a moment's notice to capture the perfect conditions. But for those who practise the sport, the wait to get out on the ice

Iceboats in front of Parkinson's Hotel, Hanlan's Point, circa 1872

From Steamer "Chief Justice Robinson" landing passengers on the ice in Toronto Bay, 1852, *from a watercolour by William Armstrong*

iceboat regattas and a number of keen sportsmen vied for trophies. Toronto iceboaters even designed and built their own boats with a special lugsail.

Up until the 1930s, when conditions were right, a fleet of iceboats would be moored just off the bottom of York Street in the city. For a modest fee iceboaters would take passengers for a thrilling ride out on the bay. Some had a good business ferrying Islanders back and forth, and even provided services delivering groceries.

In recent years, as winters got warmer and ice conditions deteriorated, the number of iceboats on Toronto Bay have decreased, but a few people, such as Albert Fulton, still keep the sport alive.

is rewarded with rides exceeding 80 kilometres an hour that are always thrilling, exciting and even dangerous.

As early as the 1840s a number of iceboats would be out on the bay as long as conditions permitted. They had to dodge skaters, fishing holes and horse-drawn sleighs, but that never seemed to deter anyone. By 1871 there were

Albert Fulton, the Toronto Island volunteer archivist, is a former high school mathematics teacher with a passion for iceboating. He used to have two iceboats, both homemade, that he kept on Toronto Island. The fastest of the two crafts had a huge sail and a red fibreglass body that held two passengers.

A Man and His Iceboat

On a cold winter afternoon with glare ice glistening in the winter sun, you find yourself crunched in beside Albert in his iceboat. A stiff breeze is just beginning to rise when the boat eases away from the shore and picks up speed. The bitter wind tears at your face; the noise of the skates thunders against the ice, inches from your body; the flimsy craft lifts one skate off the ice as gusts of wind carry it faster and faster until the boat is flying along, barely touching the ice in total exhilarating, terrifying speed.

Suddenly Albert puts the boat into a hard turn and it feels like the whole craft is about to cartwheel end over end, but somehow the skates hold their grip on the ice, and the boat is off again on another tack across the gleaming surface.

When you are finally—thankfully—back at the Island, heart thumping from the sheer frightening thrill of the ride, Albert smiles in his inscrutable way as if this is an everyday experience for him. You can't help but take a different measure of the man.

WILLIAM WARD: ISLAND LIFESAVER

By the 1830s commercial fishing was well established on the Island. The best fishing grounds were in the lake, south and west of the lighthouse where whitefish, pickerel, salmon, sturgeon and other species were found in great numbers. In time, fishermen built primitive shacks on the Island. They kept their boats on the beach, rowed out to the fishing grounds and then rowed into the city to sell their catch at the fish market on Front Street close to the present St. Lawrence Market.

The fisherman's life was a tough and hardy one. The men were in dangerous, open boats for long hours in all types of weather. Their flimsy shacks often blew down, and they received little for their efforts. Despite all of this, however, the origins of the two most famous Island families, the Wards and the Hanlans, are in this fishing community.

David Ward established himself as a fisherman in this period, and he soon had a large family living on the Island. In May of 1862 his fifteen-year-old son, William, was sailing on

William Ward, circa 1912

the bay in a small boat with five of his young sisters when the boat went over and all five of the girls drowned. William barely escaped, but this tragedy made him dedicate his life to lifesaving. In the course of his career he is credited with rescuing 164 people.

Over and over again Ward risked his life to save others. On December 7, 1868, the schooner *Jane Ann Marsh* floundered off the Island. Through the snow storm the fishermen spotted ten sailors clinging to the rigging. Twenty-year-old William Ward and Robert Berry stripped to their underwear and set out in a small skiff to attempt a rescue. Three times their boat overturned before they could get through the surf. When they finally got to the schooner they found the crew frozen to the rigging with six inches of ice. They had to beat the ice with timber until the men were free. It took seven hours, but all of the crew were saved.

On another occasion, on November 14, 1875, a furious snowy gale drove the schooner *Olive*

Toronto Harbour, 1849, from a drawing by Owen Staples

what is today Lakeshore and Manitou on Centre Island, and in 1882-83 he built a much larger hotel on the east end of the Island facing the city near Ward's Island dock, a part of the Island that came to be named after him and his family.

As well as being a hotel owner and operator Ward was appointed by the city to be the Island constable. This was not always a happy combination. Twice he was caught selling liquor, a violation of a bylaw banning the sale of alcohol on the Island, but he was so respected for his lifesaving efforts that Toronto City Council only gave him a mild reprimand.

To the end of his days William Ward remained a saver of lives. When he was well into his sixties he was still plucking people from the icy waters around Toronto Island.

Branch aground off the Island. Ward managed to swim through the frigid, heavy surf twice to get a line to the ship and save the crew. Later that day the ship *Fearless* was driven onto a sandbar off Carlaw Avenue. Rescuers tried and failed to get a line aboard. When others were ready to give up, Ward insisted that they try again and even had a fist fight with one of the other captains, but all to no avail. All night long the crew of the *Fearless* huddled in water up to their waists while the rescuers waited helplessly on shore. When dawn came Ward and others fought their way though the surf and managed to pluck the cook and five sailors off the doomed ship just before she broke up.

As he grew older William Ward became more established. In 1876 he built a small hotel at

William Ward and Robert Berry rescuing the crew of the Jane Ann Marsh, *from an engraving by Rowley W. Murphy*

NED HANLAN,
THE ROWING SENSATION

John Hanlan was another fisherman who came to the Island in the 1840s and went on to become a hotel owner and Island constable. His son, Ned, became th most famous Canadian of his day.

Island fishermen rowed their skiffs everywhere, and it is not surprising that young Ned's first toys were model boats. Legend has it that at the age of five he first rowed from the Island into the city. By the early 1870s he was working as a fisherman and helping his father around the family hotel at the western end of the Island. In 1871, at the age of 16, he entered the annual fishermen's race, but lost to William Ward.

Two years later, in 1873, Ned won his first big race when he captured the Championship of Toronto Bay, but it was the next year that his reputation was established. He defeated the well-known sculler Thomas Louden on Burlington Bay and then defeated him again in a rematch in Toronto. He went on that year to win the Lord Dufferin

Ned Hanlan (right) defeats Fred Plaisted in Toronto Bay, 15 May 1878

Ned Hanlan, circa 1876, and as an infant

Medal and the Championship of Ontario.

Rowing was an extremely popular sport in the latter part of the nineteenth century. It was closely followed by thousands of fans from all social classes and gambling on big races reached very high stakes. Ned was soon backed by a group of twenty prominent Toronto sportsmen who called themselves the Hanlan Club. They looked after the details, leaving Ned to concentrate on racing. On the side they made a lot of money gambling on their champion.

One of the things the club did was provide Ned with the best boats and equipment that money could buy. Hanlan is credited with introducing the sliding seat into the sport which allowed greater pull on the oars. This combined with his natural ability, allowed Ned to dominate the field for a number of years.

After he had defeated all the important Canadian challengers his backers arranged for him to enter in the Centennial Regatta in Philadelphia in 1876 that had the enormous purse of $800 for the winner. Ned worked in his spare time in the family hotel. The sale of alcohol on the Island was illegal at this time and Ned, like many others in the hotel trade, engaged in a little bootlegging on the side to supplement his income. The police found out about his bootlegging and issued a warrant for his arrest. For several days the champion hid out as the policemen looked for him.

Two days before he was to leave for Philadelphia the police spotted him at the Toronto Rowing Club. As they came in the front door Ned went out the back, jumped into a skiff and rowed furiously for a steamboat heading out of the harbour. He made it to the ship, climbed up a rope ladder and was off to the United States. At Philadelphia he defeated the best of the American rowers. When he returned to Toronto he was toasted by citizens and city council alike as a great hero. All charges were quietly forgotten.

The "Boy in Blue," as Ned came to be called after the colour of his racing togs, went on to win race after race in Europe, the United States and Australia. Often he would establish a commanding lead over the field and then rest on the oars, waving and blowing kisses to the girls. He was immensely popular in racing circles around the world, and wherever he raced thousands of people would come out to watch. He was Toronto's own fisherman hero whose fans adored and revered him.

The Great Reception

On July 15, 1879, word spread through the city that Ned Hanlan would be returning to Toronto aboard the lake steamer Chicora from Niagara after winning an important race in England. Three hundred passengers paid one dollar each to go across the lake from Toronto to meet him. With the band playing "See the Conquering Hero Comes," Hanlan came aboard.

Half way across the lake the Gooderham yacht *Oriole I* met the *Chicora* "with an immense spread of canvas" and led them home. Soon there were tugs, steamers and yachts surrounding them. By the time they came through the Western Gap the flotilla was three miles long.

Once in the harbour the number of small boats were so enormous that the *Chicora* had to come almost to a stop to avoid them. Ned Hanlan climbed up onto the roof of the pilot house and danced and waved at the people in the boats and the enormous throng of spectators that lined the shore from the Old Fort in the west to Yonge Street in the east. As a newspaper account of the time said: "Cheer after cheer went up, rolling along the shore, passing from wharf to wharf and housetop to housetop." It was the greatest reception ever seen before or since on Toronto Bay.

But Ned disappointed his fans. As the *Chicora* came into the dock he slipped over the side into a row boat and rowed for his beloved home on Toronto Island.

HANLAN'S POINT

Ned Hanlan was at the top of his form and the height of his popularity in 1880 when he announced that he planned to spend the princely sum of $15,000 to $16,000 to build a lavish hotel at the west end of the Island. Approvals were quickly given by Toronto City Council. Land was leased and by the summer the structure was completed. This decision led to the development of what was to become the best-known and most frequently visited part of the Island at the time, appropriately named Hanlan's Point.

By the 1880s and early '90s the city was booming, and after 1896 and through to 1913 the country experienced an unprecedented period of prosperity. The output of factories was growing rapidly as markets expanded across the country,

Hanlan's Point ferry dock

particularly in the Canadian West. Toronto had become an important financial centre. Banks were especially successful and the young Toronto Stock Exchange raised significant amounts of money for companies. Even labourers in this period had money in their pockets and were looking for new and exciting things to spend it on.

After it was built Hanlan's Hotel quickly became a distinctive landmark that attracted people by the thousands, but there were a number of other features that drew the crowds to the west end of the Island. On the lake side was (and still is) the best beach in Toronto. A bathhouse, slides and other amusements were built on the beach, and on hot summer days throngs of people came to swim and escape the heat of the city. (A city bylaw at the time stated: "Any person wearing a proper bathing dress covering the body from the neck to the knees may bathe at any time in the public waters within the city limits.")

There were special sporting events such as rowing matches held on the half-mile-long regatta course at Hanlan's. The biggest event of every season was the Dominion Day Regatta. People could rent boats or canoes and spend time paddling through the complex of lagoons. There were also baseball games and picnics.

But it was Hanlan's Point Amusement Park more than any other attraction that drew the people. By 1888 there was a merry-go-round with hand carved animals, a

Hanlan's Point Amusement Park, circa 1910

Hanlan's Point Hotel, circa 1905, from a photograph by William James

switchback railway, shooting galleries, strength-testing machines and the inevitable "freak show," featuring such performers as "the fat lady from somewhere in South Africa," a South American wild girl and a "real live Zulu with an Irish accent."

A tenting park was established at Hanlan's at the same time, and by 1888 there were up to one hundred tents of all sizes, some of them described as luxurious. The building boom of the city spilled over onto

the Island and through the 1880s and '90s the western sandbar was converted from a tenting community to cottages. However, conditions were primitive. There were outdoor privies, no running water or electricity and cooking was done over wood stoves, but the location on the sandbar looking across Humber Bay was spectacular.

For people crammed into the crowded city, with little opportunity to travel or get out into the countryside, the Island was a wonderful escape. Numerous accounts of the day emphasize the healthy effects of enjoying the Island's sunshine and fresh air. Children particularly felt the freedom of being able to explore the lagoons, meadows, beaches and those wild hidden places that young people everywhere are able to discover.

In 1890 the financier E.B. Osler formed the Toronto Ferry Company (TFC) with the objective of monopolizing the ferry service to the Island. Soon the company was doing much more than that. In 1892 the TFC took over Hanlan's Hotel and Amusement Park. Ned went on to become a

Hanlan's Point Amusement Park, circa 1910

The Trillium

On June 18, 1910, the Toronto Ferry Company launched its newest ferry, the *Trillium*, sister ship to the *Bluebell*. These two vessels were steam-driven side-wheelers, the pride of the line. Each could carry 1,300 passengers and on hot summer days they would both run to the Island filled to their limit with excited passengers.

In 1926 the city acquired the company's ferries, and the *Trillium* kept running until September 1957, almost fifty years after she was built. For a time it looked like the ferryboat would be broken up for scrap, but at the last moment a reprieve was given. The *Trillium* was towed to a mooring in a lagoon near the Island's water filtration plant, where her paint peeled and she rusted away for sixteen years.

Finally, in 1973, the city voted to refurbish the

Manuel Cappel's bicycle and Bluebell *model*

Trillium, and by May 1976 she was once again refitted and looked like new. Today she continues to ply the waters of Toronto Bay taking groups on special excursions, a fitting reminder of past glories.

The Trillium *as she appears today*

popular city alderman while the ferry company made major investments in their newly acquired assets.

The Company made profits the moment the visitor left the city. By 1896 the TFC had twelve ferries offering almost continuous service in the high season. They extended the amusement park so that there were bands playing regularly, high-wire acts, a miniature railway, photographers, peanut men, popcorn and candy apple stalls and a variety of high-profile acts designed to draw people from the city.

In 1898 the TFC got permission to dump landfill on water lots, and they increased their property from three acres to twelve

Races at Hanlan's Point stadium, 1937

point nine acres. The company then built a variety of new attractions including a giant roller coaster and a stadium that could seat 10,000 spectators. They also started the Maple Leafs of the International Baseball League, the city's first professional team, so that they would have major events to fill their stadium. There were lacrosse games, track and field meets and a variety of other events that kept fans coming through the season. Hanlan's Point in this era

was the biggest attraction of its kind in the country.

On September 8, 1903, the wooden stadium caught fire and burned to the ground, but by opening day the next year it had been rebuilt bigger and better than before. On that day, May 24, 1904, there were record-breaking crowds. So many people tried to come to Hanlan's Point that the ferries could not handle them all.

Five years later an even greater disaster struck. On August 10, 1909, a spark ignited a tent outside the Gem Theatre and quickly spread on a strong southwest wind. The fire raced through the amusement park, scattering the patrons. Clara Andras, the ticket taker at the switchback, while rushing to collect the day's receipts, got caught in the flames and lost her life.

Employees and visitors alike tried desperately to save Hanlan's Hotel, but the water pressure was too weak and the wooden structure was consumed in a frightening roar of flames. The destruction was almost complete: the amusement park, stadium, roller coaster and scores of buildings were burned to the ground. All that was left of the attractions were the merry-go-round and Durnan's boathouse. But the Toronto Ferry Company, always optimistic and resourceful, rebuilt the amusement park and stadium and by the next year they were again back in business. Only Hanlan's Hotel was not rebuilt.

Five years after the disastrous fire the First World War started. That very fall, on September 5, 1914, after the first of the troops went off to

Hanlan's Point stadium, 1910

Ferry dock at Hanlan's Point, circa 1910

war, a rangy nineteen-year-old Babe Ruth hit his first home run as a professional baseball player at the Hanlan's Point stadium. The amusement park continued to attract large numbers of soldiers and civilians, but times were changing. In 1915 the western sandbar became the first of Canada's air schools and was soon training young pilots to fight in France.

In 1922, the TFC lease on the land at Hanlan's expired and the company let the amusement park deteriorate as their negotiations with the city dragged on. In 1926, they opened Maple Leaf Stadium at the foot of Bathurst Street, transferred their baseball team to the new stadium and sold their eight remaining ferryboats and the amusement park to the city.

For the city the purchase was not a great bargain.

On the beach at Hanlan's Point, 1912, from a photograph by William James

Sunnyside Amusement Park had opened on the Lakeshore in the west end of the city and was attracting large numbers of people. The numbers were down at Hanlan's Point, and they did not even have a professional baseball team to fill their stadium. Now the Toronto Transit Commission (TTC) was operating the ferry service and the decaying amusement park. Surprisingly they did not do too badly. In the 1930s, with the incomes of many greatly diminished, Hanlan's Point drew respectable crowds as people tried to find affordable vacations. However, discussions began on alternative uses for the land.

The Lakeside Home for Little Children

As cities grew in the latter part of the nineteenth century there was an increasing concern about children's welfare. Social reformers were alarmed that boys and girls as young as eight and nine were employed in factories or worked on the streets of Toronto selling newspapers. There was also a special concern about sick and invalid children.

In 1883 the Lakeside Home for Little Children was built not far from the Island lighthouse facing west across the lake. Every summer convalescing youngsters from Sick Children's Hospital would be brought to the home with their nurses and attendants to rest and recuperate in the fresh air and sunshine.

The original building was rebuilt in 1891, but destroyed by fire in 1915. It was rebuilt again and reopened in 1917. It remained a convalescent home until 1928, when it was converted for other uses. The building was finally torn down in 1958.

Lakeside Home for Sick Children, circa 1912

In June of 1929 the Toronto Harbour Commission proposed that an airport be built at Hanlan's. There was strong opposition from the parks commissioner and others who felt that an airport would interfere with the public enjoyment of the Island. No decision on the airport was taken for the time being, but the city did approve a seaplane base. The debate continued. Other cities were building airports, and the business community felt that such a facility was a necessity in the modern age.

In 1935 an even more intense debate erupted over a proposal to extend the airport and build a tunnel to the Island. The federal government offered to build the tunnel under the Western Gap as part of R.B. Bennett's Canadian New Deal. It was approved by the city and construction underway when Mackenzie King's Liberals were elected and the tunnel was killed. But the decision on the airport was still up to the city, and on July 9, 1937, council voted the approval.

That decision totally changed Hanlan's Point. Over the next year the regatta course that had been the scene of numerous canoeing and sculling races was filled in. Land that was used for the stadium and amusement park was taken over and fifty-four houses along the western sandbar were removed. (Many of the houses were floated down to Sunfish Island, later renamed Algonquin Island, and remain there to this day.) All of that land was taken for the airport. Some houses remained until the 1950s, but then they too were demolished.

Almost immediately after the airport was completed, the Second World War had begun, and Canada allowed the Royal Norwegian Air Force to use the Island Airport as a training base. Soon it was the home of hundreds of airmen and scores of aircraft. The Island soon became filled with the sounds of buzzing war planes and machine gun fire as the pilots fired at targets out on the lake.

The Norwegians were well liked. Many attended church services on the Island and some even tried to carry on their national sport of cross-country skiing even though the flat Island must have been frustrating for them.

Originally the Island was to be the city's primary airport and Malton (the present site of Pearson International) was to be an auxiliary airport, but after the war it was obvious that the Island was not a suitable place for a major airport. Since that time it has struggled on as a general aviation airport with short range commuter flights but without much success.

For years controversy has swirled around issues such as the use of jets at the airport and a fixed link across the Western Gap. Finally, Toronto City Council voted in 1999 to build a bridge to the airport. The real question, however, is whether an airport is an appropriate use of such a magnificent piece of land, situated close to the densely populated downtown and the growing condominium community along the harbour front.

At one time Hanlan's Point was the scene of a crush of excited people as they took in the amusements or watched sporting events. Today it is the site of barren airport tarmac, and a park with few attractions and visitors. Even the beach, with its still magnificent long white sand and rolling dunes, is largely empty of people, though Toronto City Council voted in 1999 to make it a nude beach in an attempt to attract more people. Hanlan's remains a place of memories that is still a joy to explore, but it is also a place that holds the promise of what it can become.

The Toronto Island Airport

CENTRE ISLAND

Gardens at Centre Island, the former site of Manitou Road

In the early part of the nineteenth century most of the Island was a tangled wilderness cut up with shallow inlets. In 1847 the City of Toronto was given jurisdiction over the peninsula (as it was then) and immediately council members began thinking of how they could stimulate development. The City appointed a surveyor who subdivided the land into five-acre lots and then waited for the boom. Nothing much happened.

Reuben Parkinson built a hotel and wharf in 1847 near what is now Mugg's Island which quickly became a popular drinking spot. After his death, his wife Emily built a new two-story hotel on Centre Island in 1866, at the end of a

Centre Island, circa 1880, from a watercolour by Joseph T. Rolph

1,000-foot plank wharf facing the city. The hotel had deep verandas and was shaded by poplars and willows. In summer customers bowled on the grass surrounding the hotel, and in winter it was a focus of iceboating, but that was about all that went on at Centre Island.

City ownership of the Island was reconfirmed in 1867 and again the Island was surveyed in the hopes it would stimulate development. This time a promenade was designed along the southern shore that became Lakeshore Avenue, and a number of lots were created. Finally, between 1872 and '73, Mr. James Morris, a prominent lawyer, built the first cottage. By 1879 there were eight cottages, but much of Centre Island remained a wilderness.

Then, after considerable discussion, in November 1880

Canoeist in Centre Island lagoon, 1923

The Water Filtration Plant

Toronto originally drew its water from the bay, but by the middle of the nineteenth century the harbour was badly polluted, and there was concern that the city's drinking water was a danger to human health. In 1872 the city council decided to build a filtration plant on the Island and draw water from the lake.

This was a huge project for the construction engineers of the day. An intake pipe had to be laid out into the lake, and a pipe sunk across Blockhouse Bay and the Western Gap to the Mainland. By November 1875 the project was completed but two weeks later the pipe across Blockhouse Bay floated to the surface. It was another two years before the system was fully operational and the city was delivered clear, clean drinking water.

Since that time there have been several major overhauls of the system, and from 1909 to 1911 a new water treatment plant was built to increase the capacity. For well over one hundred years crews have been on the Island around the clock to maintain and monitor the system.

(the same year that Ned Hanlan built his hotel and the RCYC decided to move to the Island) city council voted to create a park at Centre Island and allocated $8,600 toward the project. Clearly, political life was changing in Toronto.

Up until this time municipal governments did little more than preside benignly over the city's affairs. By the 1880s, however, a reform movement emerged in most large centres that advocated for municipal governments to become much more active in tackling major problems.

Projects like sewage treatment plants, waterworks and street pavings were started at this time, but parks became the favourite projects in many cities in the latter part of the century. If the middle and upper classes could escape to the country and resorts, went the argument, then the rest of the population must have parks to escape the ills of the city.

The park at Centre Island was a local reflection of these ideas. Once approved the work went slowly. A new ferry dock was built, and a breakwater along the bay front and plank sidewalks were constructed. Fill was brought in from the city,

Royal Canadian Yacht Club's first Island club house, built in 1881

filling in acres of lagoons and ponds. Lawns were created and trees and gardens were planted. At the same time Long Pond was dredged and deepened to provide a rowing and canoeing course. This was one of a number of projects that reshaped the Island. Today it still has its crescent shape but little else of its original lagoons, marshes and inlets remains.

By 1886 council was still not satisfied with their new park and allocated another $120,000. There was more dredging, filling and planting. Mead's Hotel, formerly owned by Emily Parkinson, was acquired and the land was added to the park, while the structure was moved to Lakeshore and Manitou and later became the popular Pierson's Hotel. By the time the work on the park was finished in 1888, over forty acres of parkland had been created.

The new park was the pride of the city. There was room for picnics and amateur sports. John Hanlan, Ned's brother, opened a boat rental business on the south side of Long Pond in 1891. Later, a bandstand was built for concerts and in 1895 a ferris wheel was erected.

Yonge Street wharf, 1910, from a photograph by William James

While Hanlan's had the big amusement park which attracted large crowds, Centre Island Park was a more relaxed place. Picnic spots were in such great demand by the 1890s that reservations had to be made a year in advance. One visitor in 1894 wrote:

> *The family man, or more sedate citizen, will go to the Island Park where he can lie on the grass and watch the children play or stroll over to the promenade and enjoy the fresh lake breezes.*

The creation of the park and other improvements, such as roads, encouraged the development of Centre Island's cottage community. Another stimulus was the opening of the new RCYC clubhouse in 1881. As many members wanted to be close to their boats and the social life at the club, an increasing number of club members took leases on land and built cottages.

Residential developments in parks were common at that time, and few people saw a conflict between private property and public interest. The city owned the land and charged a ground rent to cottagers. It was felt that this rent helped to support the public areas, and that the houses did not interfere with the enjoyment of the beaches and public spaces.

The first big building boom came in 1881 and by 1885 there were over fifty summer residences east of the filtering plant. Among them was a cottage overlooking the lake built by George Gooderham, a member of one of the wealthiest families in the city, and an ardent yachtsman. In 1884 William Clark opened a store on Manitou Road, and soon he was delivering goods all over the Island. By the time the park opened in 1888 the summer population of the Island

St. Andrew's-by-the-Lake

In 1882 the Anglican bishop, Arthur Sweatman, decided that a church was needed to serve the growing Island community. A committee was put together, funds were raised and a site was chosen. On Sunday, July 27, 1884 St. Andrew's-by-the-Lake opened at the corner of Cherokee and Lakeshore. Right beside it was the bishop's own cottage that he named "Happy-Go-Lucky."

For over one hundred years the church and a succession of ministers have served the Island community. In 1895 the church was enlarged and in 1960, when the Centre Island community was demolished, it was moved to its present location beside the lagoon on Centre Island. The church is still used regularly by Island residents, members of the yacht clubs and visitors from the city.

St. Andrew's is a very pretty building built of white

St. Andrew's-by-the-Lake

clapboard and brown trim with a small bell tower over the entrance. Inside, the walls and vaulted ceiling are lined with tongue and groove fir that give it a dark, warm, solemn effect. There are several beautiful stained glass windows created by W.T. Lyon and produced in his glassworks on Church Street in Toronto.

Main Street, Centre Island, Toronto, Canada

Manitou Road, circa 1910

was over 1,000 people. With the improved ferry service, new stores, a church, and a school, life on Centre Island was beginning to change.

Development continued apace in the period leading up to the First World War. The city developed another thirty-six acres on Olympic Island as parkland and continued to give out leases to cottagers. Many members of prominent Toronto families built at Centre Island including: Arthur L. Massey, a member of the family who owned the farm implement manufacturing company, E.J. Lennox, the architect of Old City Hall and Casa Loma and Casimir Gzowski Jr., of the well-known railway-building and manufacturing family.

The commercial development along Manitou Road, or

The Massey cottage, circa 1940

where young people could sleep two and three to a room. Over the summer there were always events going on: bonfires on the beach, sing songs, baseball games, canoe races and social events at the yacht and canoe clubs. There were general stores, ice cream parlours, a meat market, laundries, restaurants, dairies and, for those who could afford them, elegant meals at the handsome Pierson's Hotel.

Development slowed through the First World War, but as soon as the war ended Centre Island was in full swing again. In 1921 Fred Ginn built his "Casino" dance pavilion on Manitou Road, across from Pierson's Hotel, with "the best dance floor in the city." The jazz age bands attracted Islanders and city folk to dances featuring the Charleston, fox trot and slow romantic numbers.

Islanders devoted hours of time to the care of their cottages, and in time most of these structures developed a certain grace and comfortable charm. Many cottages had big verandas that wrapped around two or more sides and almost all of them had beautiful gardens with a profusion of flowers creeping along the fences and around the doorways. There was pride in the community. People held fond memories of previous summers and anticipated the next with excitement.

In the latter part of the 1930s the Island's winter population began to grow slowly after the *Ned Hanlan*, an

the "Main Drag" as it was known, became the focus of Centre Island life. At times Manitou Road was so crowded that people jostled each other for space. There was even fear that there would be serious accidents because of the growing bicycle population.

The social life was made up of a wide mix of cottagers on Toronto Island. A saying of the day was that the Island was "for the Masseys and the masses." There were elegant summer mansions, small one-story cottages and boarding houses

Pierson's Hotel, circa 1930

eighty-foot steam-powered tug, was put into service. The tug could crush through the thickest ice, and, though passengers often had to huddle out on the deck in bitter wind, the problem of winter transportation had been partly solved.

It was during the Second World War when Centre Island began to change into a year-round community. People came to Toronto from across the country to work in the war industries. By 1943 there was a serious housing shortage. The city improved the winter services on the Island and encouraged

The Ned Hanlan *serving as an Island ferry in winter*

people to winterize their cottages so that they could be used throughout the year. By 1945 it is estimated the Island population had grown to 2,000 in the winter and 10,000 in the summer.

After the war the housing crisis continued, and even more people came to live on the Island year round. Stores stayed open. The Manitou Hotel became the gathering place for beer-drinking adults as well as teenagers eager to hear the latest songs on the juke box. There was a Legion Hall, and in 1950 both a bowling alley and a 700-seat movie theatre opened. Baseball was the summer sport of choice, and in the winter, games of pick-up hockey were played on the frozen lagoons. As well, people made their own entertainment. There was carolling at Christmas, euchre parties and the "Ferryboat Follies" talent show where anyone could get up to entertain their neighbours.

But all of this was soon to come to an end. When the

The Manitou Hotel, circa 1925

Metropolitan Toronto level of government was established in 1953 the first Metro chairman, Fred Gardiner, favoured large-scale, highly visible projects. He once said: "Plans, plans, we've got a million plans. Let's get the goddamn shovels in the ground." He was a man of his times that believed in an active government, and he certainly led one.

Four months after his appointment he proposed the transfer of all the Island land to Metro. Gardiner did not say what he wanted to do once he gained control, and in fact he gave hints that he supported the retention of the existing housing at least until 1966 if not longer. But once the land was transferred decisions were then in the hands of a council dominated by suburban constituents who did not much care what happened to the Island and were generally in favour of creating parks as long as it did not disturb their own constituents.

With all the ensuing political indecision the Island began to change and lose some of its vitality. The number of visitors were down, the hotels and boarding houses did not have the same number of tenants, and the businesses along Manitou were not doing well. When Tommy Thompson, the new Metro parks commissioner, said that "existing housing on the Island (was) of little value and should be removed," many in the city tended to agree with him. Gardiner and his political friends argued that the Island should be developed simply with plenty of open space and the media and the public seemed to agree with him. To them the Island was a rather messy place, and in the political environment of the 1950s, where suburban values dominated, it was time to clean up and impose some order.

The political decision to demolish the Island community happened with blinding speed that made it almost impossible for the residents to react. On May 25, 1955 the City of Toronto agreed to transfer all of its land to Metro. Even before Metro officially took title, on January 1, 1956, bulldozers began to tear down the houses that had been vacated. People were confused and demoralized, and did not know where to turn for help. In the end the Islanders hardly put up a fight, concentrating on getting the best settlement for themselves. This is how Sally Gibson, the writer, described it:

> *The demolition program picked up speed in the fall and winter of 1956-57, as the Parks Department prepared to raze and raise a large part of Centre. Great steel-clawed backhoe machines rumbled across lawns and backyards, tearing and ripping their way through fragile wooden reminders of a bygone era. Smoke curled upward into the grey winter sky, as the piles of splintered wood were set on fire. Then the bulldozers pushed earth over the dying embers of a dying community, leaving "only mounds of earth where homes once stood." And the Metro workmen moved on to the next target, and the next, and the next.*

By September 1960 some twenty stores and 261 houses had been torn down. Manitou Road, the "Main Drag" that

Fountain at the Flower Gardens

The Island Public and Nature School

The Island school has reflected the fortunes of the community more accurately than any other institution. In the early 1880s Katherine Durnan, the wife of the lighthouse keeper, began teaching Island children in her home. The community grew rapidly, and in 1888 a one-room schoolhouse with seventeen students ranging from grades one to nine opened near the lighthouse.

Enrolment grew slowly until 1945 and then, as more and more families made the Island their permanent home, the school population exploded. In 1954 it reached its peak of 587 students. With the demolition of the houses on Hanlan's Point and Centre Island, the numbers dropped dramatically, but in recent years enrolment has stabilized as many students have come to the Island Public School from the city's Harbourfront community. In 1998-99 there were 123 students in classes from kindergarten to grades six. About sixty percent of the students come from the city and forty percent from the Island community.

In 1964 the Board of Education established a special program called the Island Public Nature Science School. Students in grades five and six from city schools come to the Island and live at the school for an entire week for a special course designed to encourage an appreciation and knowledge about nature.

On February 1, 1999 the Island Public School moved into a new school on Centre Island. It is a modern, well-equipped, state-of-the-art facility that is in keeping with the Island's natural setting.

A Greener and Happier Place

Alexander Ross, *The Telegram*,
July 31, 1965

For me Manitou Road has all the mythic connotations of a Via Veneto or Cannery Row. It was a sweet raffish thoroughfare that looked like a stage set from High Noon. It had an incredible hotel run by a man who'd once been married to Tallulah Bankhead or Joan Leslie or somebody, a sloppy old firehall and an assortment of flyblown general stores.

Most of Manitou's permanent residents were escapees of one sort or another: from bad marriages, from failure, from city living, but they had each other. They had the Island, and they had developed a unique, and to me, admirable style of life. It was a neighbourhood, something that may be going out of style, and now it has been replaced by a lot of municipal potted plants.

I don't want to dwell on the glories of the Island that used to be, except to record one fact that might be relevant to city planners. My two summers on the Island constituted the happiest period of my life. There were bicycle rides to the yacht clubs, willow trees overhanging the canals, girls who sometimes missed the last water-taxi to the mainland, and Island children who, despite their parent's slum income, grew up beautifully in a sane and lovely environment. And there are thousands of ex-Islanders who carry this same vision around with them, of a place that was greener and happier than any other place they ever knew.

Manitou Road, 1954

of the Centre Island community is still mourned by those old enough to remember. The Island's main use is on summer weekends when large family groups stream over by the thousands. Many of the visitors are people from the inner city who indeed come for the fresh air that the enormous park offers, and a substantial number are immigrant families who are amazed that Canada has such large parks close to the downtown of its cities.

At Centre Island there are picnics by the dozens during the summer, baseball games, volleyball, Frisbee, golf and soccer. It is still a space where kids can explore the hidden places, and adults can sit on the shore of the lake, looking toward the horizon, as they marvel at the water and the big sky.

Children on the Centre Island ferry boat

had teemed with creative, chaotic anarchy, had been converted into a neatly trimmed formal flower garden. It became in the eyes of many as appealing as "a plastic pie plate." Acres and acres of empty green parkland replaced Island houses.

Other attractions have been added since the destruction of the community. In 1959 a model farm for kids was opened, and in 1966 a children's amusement park was added. For many, however, Centre Island was simply not the same. The old vibrant community with its exciting alternative lifestyles was gone, replaced by an example of sterile municipal neatness.

Today, over forty years after these events, the demolition

Children in the Amusement Park

AN ISLAND OF FESTIVALS

Centre Island Park has long been a place for large events of various sorts. Up until the end of the 1940s company picnics were the order of the day. Activities would normally include three-legged races and wheelbarrow races for the kids, egg in the spoon races for the ladies and tug of war for the men. The events would conclude with a huge meal of ham, coleslaw and the inevitable potato salad spread out on long tables in the park. Many people in Toronto still have fond memories of such events.

Dragon Boat Races

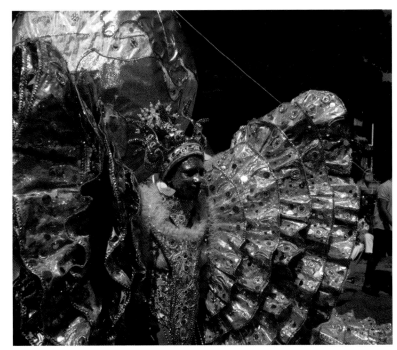

Caribana festivities

Centre Island was always a popular place for political leaders to meet their supporters, or prospective supporters. Sir John A. Macdonald, a man who was always ready for a social occasion, attended more than one boating and rowing event with his affluent friends at the yacht club. Pierre and Margaret Trudeau were on Centre Island in 1974 campaigning at a picnic during the federal election of that year. And numbers of more modest politicians have also hosted picnics or barbecues for their workers and supporters on the Island.

In recent years the big park at Centre Island has been the favourite venue for a variety of festivals. In 1968 the Mariposa Folk Festival was first held on Olympic Island. It was a great success with dozens of stars, thousands of visitors and long waits for the ferries. For several years the festival was held on the Island and every year the numbers grew larger. In 1970 over 85,000 fans paid admission and several swam across the lagoon to crash the event. Finally success was too great for the Island facilities to handle and the organizers moved the festival to Barrie.

The CHIN picnic, starting in 1968 and for many years

after, was held on Olympic Island. This festival, hosted by a local radio station, reached a large number of new Canadians and reflected, perhaps better than any other event held on the Island, the multi-ethnic nature of Toronto. Every year thousands of participants were on hand for the crowning of Miss Bikini, spaghetti-eating contests and musical acts. Politicians, too, were always there for that universal political pastime—pressing the flesh.

Caribana, the great West Indian festival, was first held in Toronto in 1967, and it has been held on the first weekend in August every year since. The best-known part of the festival is the annual parade through the streets of Toronto featuring the fantastic costumes typical of West Indian carnivals. In the evening a huge concert is held on Olympic Island with music from the Caribbean Islands, attracting thousands of young people.

The most recent addition to the list of festivals is the annual Dragon Boat Races that are held on Long Pond at Centre Island. This is an event organized by the Chinese community of Toronto, but which attracts competitors and spectators from across the city. They come to participate in the races or just to enjoy the food and culture from East Asia.

WARD'S AND ALGONQUIN

The community at Ward's and Algonquin developed more slowly than other parts of the Island. In 1882, when Hanlan's was a booming resort, and the park was under construction at Centre, Wiman's Baths, or change house, was built at Ward's. To encourage other development the city planted trees, filled ponds and laid boardwalks.

The next year William Ward built his hotel near the ferry docks facing north toward the city. It was a three-story structure with a tower and long, deep verandas. Although it was not nearly as grand a hotel as Ned Hanlan's, it was a success as a drinking establishment, despite a bylaw banning the sale of alcohol on the Island. The hotel

Ward's Hotel, 1954

From Centre to Ward's by Boardwalk

Stretching from Ward's to Centre Islands is a two-and-a-half-kilometre boardwalk that follows the seawall on the very edge of Lake Ontario. It is busiest on sunny summer afternoons, when it is the scene of strolling couples, groups struggling with the Island's unique four-wheeled bikes or families with kids, strollers and grandparents.

But there can be some very special moments along the walk. In the winter, waves smashing over the seawall during a storm will freeze on the trees, making a glistening fairyland by the next morning. Perhaps the most beautiful time is late on hot summer nights, when the sky is clear and all is quiet. The silver moon glistens on the surface of the lake, while countless stars gleam in the sky. On the far distant shore the lights from St. Catharines and Niagara Falls glow against the horizon, and out on the lake sailboats and tour boats slowly drift through the water as they head for the harbour. These are truly the Island's most magical moments.

On the boardwalk

remained in use until it was torn down in the 1960s.

Ward's Island was undeveloped until after the turn of the century. A Toronto Island Guide, published in 1894, used flowery prose to describe it.

2 Withrow Street, Ward's Island

The melancholy soul who pines for solitude or the poet whose fervour radiates from him with such intensity to scorch the vegetation, or the student who wants a quiet nook free from distraction, will go to Ward's and lounge on the breakwater and commune with the wild waves.

Around the turn of the century the buildings of Wiman's Baths were converted into apartments and a section of this property was set aside for camping. A tenting community had existed for some time at Hanlan's but the city began to restrict this site, and ultimately it was closed. Many of the tenters migrated down to Ward's. By 1904 there were ten tents, and by 1906 there were twenty-eight. Then there was an explosion

Picnic, circa 1940

Simpson's Cottages

In the 1930s, after approval was given by the city to build permanent structures on Ward's Island, Simpson's Department Store began selling prefab cottages to Islanders. The price varied from $311.00 to $449.50 depending on the size and model.

These were basic structures with no basements or insulation, but for the Ward's Islanders, with very small lots and no possibility of putting in a basement because of the water table, they were just right.

Although many have been altered, the outline of the Simpson's cottages can be seen in many of the homes on Ward's to this day.

Simpson's cottage ad, 1933

of population. In 1912 it is estimated that there were 685 campers who summered on the east end of the Island.

The tenters at Ward's were not the affluent cottage dwellers of Centre Island. They tended to be craftsmen or unskilled workers looking for an affordable summer holiday for their family. From their tents, the members of the family who worked could commute into the city while the rest of the family could enjoy the freedom of the outdoors on the Island.

Tent city, 1911

Conditions were primitive in the tenting community. There was no city water until 1906, and even then people had to use communal water facets and lavatories. Tents were lit by coal oil lanterns. People used root cellars and cooked over open fires. Wind was a special problem. In strong gales people literally held onto their tents and belongings so they would not blow away. In order to combat the wind poplar trees were planted. But despite these problems the tenters were enthusiastic about their summers on the Island. Not only was it a chance to get away, but it was affordable. Tents did not cost very much and rent on the land in the period prior to the First World War was only fifteen to twenty dollars a season.

In time, the city slowly began to make improvements. Ponds on Ward's were filled. In 1912 a new bathhouse and lifesaving station were opened on Ward's beach, and in 1913 streets were laid out. The site was graded, brush was removed, and lights were strung. Water pipes were laid and

15 Sixth Street, Ward's Island

six-foot-wide plank sidewalks were put down. In 1916 the community was laid out in streets much like it exists today.

The Ward's Island Association (WIA) was established in 1913 to preside over the social life of the community. There was dancing, euchre, sports days for the kids, tennis, bowling, sailing and rowing. Baseball became such a passion that there were games almost every night. All summer long there was a supervised children's program. Many learned to swim, sail and row in this program and a few became famous sportsmen like Jack Guest, a world-class rower.

In 1906 the city began to make improvements to Sunfish Island (later renamed Algonquin). It was enlarged, using sand suckers that brought up material from the bottom of the bay. In 1918 the YMCA established a camp for working boys on Sunfish, and that summer sixty-five boys lived in tents out on the sandbar. The camp ran for

19 Fourth Street, Ward's Island

several years despite the lack of trees and lavatories. In 1921 the Queen City Yacht Club joined the YMCA on Sunfish and built their clubhouse on the east end of the Island with moorings in the lagoon. The club remains there to this day.

The 1920s was the "golden age of tent life on Ward's Island," as Sally Gibson called it. The modest incomes of people were beginning to improve. Tents were getting larger and wooden tarpaper structures were used as cooking shacks. There were a few disputes about noise, but generally the "Wardsies" got along pretty well together. The WIA organized the first Gala Day on the August long weekend of 1921. (Gala Day has been held on this weekend every year since.) Everyone was busy all summer long with sporting events, talent shows and just lazing about. Best of all, ferry service improved so that the last boat to Ward's was now at eleven.

11 Oneida Avenue, Algonquin Island

It was in 1931 that Toronto City Council finally agreed to allow permanent structures to replace the tents on Ward's Island, but the city laid down strict regulations. The buildings could be no more than 840 square feet, had to have electricity and would have to be maintained in a satisfactory condition. Furthermore, no dogs or boisterous behaviour were allowed. By 1937 over 130 cottages had been built and only thirty-two campsites remained. The rest disappeared in the 1940s. In August 1937 the WIA allotted $2,600 to build a clubhouse and by the next spring it was completed. (It is still a well-used building where dances and other events are held. In recent years it has housed a popular summer café.)

Sunfish Island remained a barren sandbar until the decision to build the Island Airport at Hanlan's Point at the end of the 1930s changed all of that. The airport was to displace scores of cottages. After extensive discussions the city agreed to open Sunfish to development and float down the cottages. That fall the Parks Department added more fill to the sandbar and built a bridge across to Ward's Island. The houses were moved in two stages to their new sites and by mid-June of 1938 thirty-one houses had arrived and were placed on lots around the periphery of the newly named Algonquin Island. That summer the city laid sidewalks, buried water lines and planted trees, but to many the Island "looked like a desert" until the trees grew.

Island Transportation: The Bicycle

The policy of the Island as a car-free community was not so much a conscious political decision as it was a practice that just emerged. Distances are short, and there is no fixed link across to the mainland, so it made sense to establish the rule that only service vehicles would be allowed. But this rule has stamped an indelible character on the Island and its people.

Bicycles are the basic transportation for everyone. In the heyday of Centre Island, Manitou Road was a thicket of bikes leaning against every conceivable tree, pole and building. Today every Islander, young and old, has their bicycle that they use in all seasons and all types of weather. Many commute to work on them in the city. On Saturday mornings Islanders by the dozens ride to do their shopping at St. Lawrence Market, and the stories are legion of the biggest, the most delicate or the most awkward load that people have carried on their bikes.

But more than this, the rule of a car-free community influences the way Islanders relate to one another. People do not have the same concern about safety as others in the city. Adults talk to their neighbours on the street. Kids run free. It is a walking, cycling community that gives everything a more human scale.

Islander Murray Darrah and his bicycle

In total, there were 110 lots created on Algonquin Island. By the beginning of the Second World War only about forty of them were occupied. After the war the housing shortage stimulated development. Some returning veterans used their housing grants to build houses, and for a time Algonquin was the scene of scores of construction sites. The other important development occured in 1951 when the Algonquin Island Association (AIA) clubhouse was built. Unlike its WIA cousin it was insulated and could be used in winter.

In the period after the war Ward's and Algonquin followed the pattern of Centre and Hanlan's Islands. Up until the war Fram Ward, the Island firechief and grandson of William, and his family were the only ones who wintered over on Ward's Island, but the acute housing shortage led to the winterizing of cottages. Soon most of the houses on both Islands were occupied year round. The resulting neighbourhood was made up of residents with a rich social life and a deep attachment to their community. Like the people at Centre Island they were completely unprepared for the political decisions that would change their lives.

Algonquin Island Association clubhouse

THE FIGHT FOR HOME AND COMMUNITY

By 1960 Metro bulldozers had done their work of demolishing the communities of Hanlan's and Centre. Residents of Ward's and Algonquin were demoralized and confused. They wanted to stay on the Island, but how could they stop this powerful political machine from sweeping them aside as well?

In 1963 the Metro parks commissioner, Tommy Thompson, unveiled a twelve-million-dollar plan for all

Islanders wait for the sheriff, 28 July 1980

housing on the Island to be removed by 1968. The plan outlined various developments such as golf courses, sports lands and amusement parks. The entire Island, in his vision, was to be totally devoted to public use and all private housing was to be removed.

There were objections to the plan by groups in the city, and Islanders took this opportunity to outline their own opposition. They hired a prominent lawyer and planner and gave a strong argument that the Island should be left essentially as it was. In the end there was a delay, but the Thompson plan was endorsed by Metro Council.

Although they had lost this skirmish, the opponents had demonstrated an emerging political confidence among Islanders. There were other changes. Several people from Hanlan's and Centre, who were determined to stay on the Island, managed to get houses on Ward's and Algonquin. New people were coming to the Island who were familiar with political activity through the anti-Vietnam War and

student movements. Together these people had extensive political contacts and skills, and they were determined to mount an opposition.

Islanders had been thrown on the defensive. They had to take the offence or they would be buried in Thompson's argument of full public access. Gradually a new set of arguments and strategies emerged.

It was not so much that they were against the concept of public ownership, Islanders argued, but they were opposed to the destruction of their community. The public already had full access to a 820-acre park that was largely vacant for much of the year. Why did they need the remaining forty acres occupied by the Ward's and Algonquin communities? What's more, the Island was a unique community that enhanced the public's enjoyment.

Having the arguments was only the first step. The next was to develop an effective campaign that would put them on the offence. In 1964, the year after Thompson rolled out

Sign at the Ward's Island clubhouse, 1978

Sam McBride

In a community of colourful characters no Islander became better known than Sam McBride. A lumber merchant by occupation, Sam was one of the first tenters on Ward's Island, and he continued to spend his summers there for the rest of his life.

First elected to Toronto City Council in 1905, Sam soon developed a reputation as one of the most boisterous, if not uncontrollable, members of that traditionally undisciplined political body. Once he got into a fist fight with a fellow alderman and received a black eye. On another occasion he threw a can of beans at a fellow politician and dented the decorative woodwork in the council chambers. At both Island sporting events and city council meetings his booming voice could be heard shouting for the side he supported.

Sam could always be depended on to support Island issues. He was the political force behind efforts to improve Island services and facilities. In 1928 and again in 1929 he was elected the mayor of Toronto. In 1930 he lost but was soon back on council letting his opinions be known. After his successful campaign against the tunnel to the Island under the Western Gap, Sam was again elected mayor in 1935, but the next year he fell ill and died. His funeral was one of the biggest ever seen in the city.

In 1939 a new ferryboat was named in McBride's honour. It continues to ply the waters of the bay and take people to his favourite place— Toronto Island.

his plan, Islanders launched their "Save Island Homes" campaign. This remained their slogan, with variations, for the duration of the fight. The political message that the slogan captured was easy to understand. It meant: save the Island community from the destruction advocated by politicians. In the coming years of struggle that simple

message was the Islanders' greatest weapon.

But the other side also had a strategy. Metro Chairman William Allen and Commissioner Tommy Thompson used the media to create the impression that Islanders lived in a slum with no proper heating, no toilets and defective wiring. Islanders counterattacked by arguing that this was a historical, unique, affordable community worth saving. Individuals hosted politicians on the Island to let them see the houses and talk to the people.

The battle lines had been drawn. This was a struggle between a small community of residents and big government, between an old neighbourhood with all its messiness and the neat and tidy middle class, and, finally, a struggle between the downtown core of the city and the suburbs.

By the fall of 1966 there were only forty-four homeowners along Lakeshore leading to Ward's who would receive compensation when their houses were taken. The rest of the houses were on leases and no compensation would be paid. In May of 1967 the issue to expropriate and demolish the forty-four houses came before Metro Council. After an emotional debate the council vote was tied: fourteen to fourteen. Chairman Allen broke the tie by voting for demolition. The motion called for the rest of the houses to be cleared by August 1970.

There was understandable bitterness in the community as the forty-four houses were bulldozed, but some concluded that the vote had been so close it showed that victory was a possibility. On July 30, 1969, WIA Chairman Peter Gzowski (who later went on to become a media superstar) and AIA Chairman Mark Harrison called a meeting to propose forming a resident's association to spearhead the opposition to the Metro bulldozers. The meeting was packed and response was overwhelmingly enthusiastic. Islanders had made the decision to resist Metro with every means at their disposal. Originally the association was called the Island Resident's Association, the IRA, but soon the Irish troubles convinced people to change it to TIRA—Toronto Island Residents' Association.

Not only was the political mood changing on the Island, but the December 1969 election saw a new style of municipal politician in the city. John Sewell, Karl Jaffery, David Crombie and William Kilbourn were all first elected to Toronto City Council that year. They supported neighbourhoods and were highly critical of the old-style politicians who worked closely with the development industry. In 1972 a loose group of political allies called "The Reform Slate," gained control of council and David Crombie was elected mayor.

There were small but important victories for TIRA in those years as the orders for demolition were delayed. Then, dramatically, in November 1973 a city report recommended that the Island community be preserved and become another neighbourhood. The report was adopted overwhelmingly by city council with a vote of seventeen to two. Islanders were ecstatic, but the fight was far from over. Control of the Island rested with Metro Council, not the city. Paul Godfrey was now the Metro chairman, and he was determined to clear the Island for a park. Metro voted to terminate the leases on Ward's and Algonquin by twenty to twelve.

Islanders responded with a concerted effort to win the public to their cause. City people were invited to the Island Winter Carnival. Delegations were sent to suburban community groups to gain support. Always the slogan was repeated: "Save Island Homes," but the campaign seemed to do little good. The political situation at Metro Council had polarized between the city and the suburbs, and there were no significant shifts.

TIRA launched a legal challenge against the termination of the leases and focused their political efforts on Queen's Park. A minority Conservative government, led by Bill Davis, had been elected. The local member, Larry Grossman, was sympathetic to the Island cause, but he had to convince the government and that was difficult. The legal case was lost, and six Island homes were served with "writs of possession." Metro was getting ready to act.

The Island community prepared for civil disobedience. The Home Guard was formed—a unit wearing bright yellow hard hats ready to occupy any house that was about to be taken by the sheriff. War games were held to test the defences. An air raid siren was installed on the top of the WIA clubhouse, ready to shriek out a warning whenever danger arose, and Toronto Island Radio Network, TIRN, was set up with Kay Walker, the Island anchor woman, known to bark out orders so loudly she hardly needed a radio.

Meanwhile provincial politicians tried to negotiate with Metro, but Paul Godfrey would not be moved. The province suggested that Islanders be allowed to stay in their homes for as long as they lived in them and then their homes would be torn down. TIRA rejected this solution as one of "attrition"—the slow death of the community. Finally, the provincial government appointed Barry Swadron to head a "Commission of Inquiry into the Toronto Islands."

Despite the province, Metro was determined to push ahead. By July 1980 all avenues of appeal had been exhausted, and they appeared to be ready to act to seize the houses. The Home Guard was on twenty-four hour alert; everyone knew it was down to the final hours.

Monday, July 28, was a drizzly summer day. Word suddenly came from an inside source that the sheriff was coming. The phone chain was activated. No matter where they were in the city, or what they were doing, Islanders and their supporters rushed down to the waterfront. There, a virtual flotilla was waiting—the "Island Navy"—to take everybody across the water to defend their homes.

By midday close to 1,000 people, adults and children, were gathered at the Algonquin Bridge along with media from most of the Toronto and national news organizations. A huge banner read "Save us Bill Davis," giving the political message that only the premier of the province could save the Island community now.

At three-thirty p.m. the acting sheriff arrived with his delegation in two cars. The crowd linked arms and sang "We Shall Not Be Moved." Liz Amer and Ron Mazza, TIRA co-chairs, talked to the sheriff and got him to agree to withdraw while a minor matter of the writs was settled. With the sheriff staff leaving, the Islanders broke into pandemonium. It seemed as though a complete victory had been won.

Robert Fulford captured the spirit and memory of the moment better than anyone:

Perhaps it didn't actually change anything. Perhaps the community would have been saved anyway. But in the mythology of the Island — that most romantic slice of Toronto, that embattled sandbar bohemia in the bay — the Day of the Bridge, July 28, 1980, was the most marvelous of days, the day when Islanders all stood firm in the rain and saved their homes and their souls, saved them from the bulldozers and the barbarians in the Metro Parks Department.

The sheriff did not return, but there were many struggles yet to come. The province introduced legislation to stay the writs. When the Swadron Report was issued it recommended that the community be allowed to stay for twenty-five years, until July 31, 2005. Metro was to retain ownership of the land but lease it to the city for "fair market value."

There were still major problems. A legal decision gave ownership of the houses to Metro. Islanders were furious. It was like being delivered into the arms of their enemies. TIRA tried to resolve the issue, but by that time there was little political will, even at the City of Toronto.

This complicated issue was eventually resolved by the NDP government in 1993 with Bill 61. The legislation created the Toronto Island Land Trust, TILT, to administer the land. The houses became the property of the occupants, a one-time payment was made by Islanders for a ninety-nine year lease on the land and restrictions were made on resale so that profit could not be made on the land or the houses.

After the Harris Conservative government came to power in 1995, it appeared that the deal would be cancelled, and the struggle to save Island homes would be fought all over again, but saner heads prevailed. The government cancelled a co-op of 110 units, but Islanders were allowed to build twelve new homes within the existing envelope of the community.

As the heat around these issues gradually subsided the feeling among most Islanders was more of relief than pride over their victory in the difficult struggle to save their community. In the end the settlement represents a good Canadian compromise that means a victory for everyone. The Island Park is strengthened by the community adjacent to it, and a unique, historical neighbourhood was saved— one that contributes enormously to the richness and diversity of the city.

Freighter and ferry in the harbour

The Islanders and the Ferryboats

For Islanders the ferries are more than a system of transportation; they are the place where they meet their friends exchange news and gossip. Like members had the character of political rallies aimed at cheering on the troops. When a victory was won the celebration would start on the boat ride home, and in the face of defeat neighbours would reassure each other that in the long run justice was on their side.

Island ferries at the Bay Street wharf, 1912. Right: Bay Street docks today

of any small community, Islanders live semi-public lives, but over and over again the talk comes back to politics: "What are they trying to do to us at City Hall?" "Can we count on the province for support?" "Who is the best person to lobby the Mayor?"

When the fight to save the Island community was at its height in the '70s and '80s ferry rides sometimes

"Perhaps," an Islander recently speculated, "we never would have won the battle for the community if it wasn't for the ferryboat rides."

A Special Place to Live

9 Channel Avenue, Ward's Island

Today, life on the Island has regained normality. No longer do people fear the bulldozers. The Home Guard has been disbanded, the siren on top of the WIA clubhouse, it has not been heard in years.

But life on the Island has continued to be influenced by political events. There has been a flurry of construction since the legislation was passed giving security to the community, as previously Islanders could not get building

Converted office shed, Algonquin Island

Garden, 3 Seneca Avenue, Algonquin Island

permits. Many smuggled construction material like rum runners illegally transporting liquor. Today homeowners can get permits, like everyone else in the city. There has been construction of homes and even a new school has been built. All of this has given new life and vitality to the community.

Most of the building that has gone on has respected the unique character of the Island. The houses are small, particularly on Ward's. People are conscious that they should not encroach on their neighbours. There has been some change: new siding has been added here, a dormer or a deck there, but much of the work has been inside. Lofts have been built under the eves, kitchens have been modernized and, in some cases, modest second floors have been added.

On Algonquin Island the lots are bigger, but again the new buildings have respected the character of the community. As kids grow into teenagers small Island homes become cramped. The solution for a number of families has been to winterize an old shed where the young person can live with some semblance of privacy. Other sheds have been converted

Art garden, 32 Omaha Avenue, Algonquin Island

Wildlife

There is a great variety of wildlife on the land and in the waters around the Island that changes with the seasons.

Canadian geese and various ducks stay all year long. These are hardy birds able to withstand the pressures of boats and people.

In spring the Island is a flyway for birds returning from the south. Robins arrive not long after the frost leaves the ground, followed by a profusion of songbirds of various species flitting through the trees and bushes.

By summer the night herons sit in tall trees by day. At night they find a perch at the water's edge on a rock or a dead tree and wait to catch frogs or minnows. During the day the seagulls come over from the Leslie Street Spit to prance up and down the beaches looking for food.

One of the spectacular events of early September is the migration of monarch butterflies passing through the Island as they head to their wintering grounds in Mexico. It is remarkable that such fragile, delicate things can travel such distances.

In winter the Arctic water birds return from the far North to forage for food in the open waters of the bay and Lake Ontario. They are joined by white trumpeter swans with long graceful necks.

The waters around the Island once again teem with fish. Chinook salmon are caught in increasing numbers. The whitefish have disappeared but there are pike, pickerel, catfish and other species.

On the land a number of animals live on the Island year round such as harmless garter snakes, muskrats, racoons, painted and snapping turtles, frogs and toads. A beaver recently made its home by the RCYC moorings.

Other animals are more elusive. Families of fox have wintered on the Island in recent years, and one year a lone coyote was often spotted loping along the frozen lagoons. No one knows for sure, but it is thought that they come across the ice from the Leslie Street Spit in the winter, looking for new hunting grounds.

into offices for family members working out of the home.

Gardens are a particularly important means of expression for Islanders. August weekends feature garden tours, but it is worth coming to look at the gardens at any time in the summer. On Ward's the lots are so small that many people devote their entire space to flowers and shrubs, creating tight, urban-style gardens. Algonquin has more extensive space and gardens tend to spread with more variety and profusion.

Although Island living provides an ideal rustic retreat from the city, there are decided drawbacks. Everything, from groceries to furniture, has to be hauled over on carts or bicycles. The last boat at eleven-thirty at night is a curfew or a blessing depending on the point of view. Most young people in their late teens and early twenties miss the last boat so often that they either move into town or spend a lot of money on water taxis. On the other hand, some parents appreciate the deadline set by the ferry.

Islander Grahame Beakhurst in his garden, Ward's Island

Rock Garden, 11 Oneida Avenue, Algonquin Island

Islanders are a mixed lot. Admittedly it is a very Waspish community, but there is a great variety of ages and incomes. Island children have a friendly openness with adults because they live in a safe community with no cars and little crime. Older people are helped to stay in their homes for as long as possible. Islanders tend to draw their friends from a wide social spectrum. Lawyers hang out with artists; labourers are friendly with university professors; teenagers often help older people. In that sense it is an integrated community where people look after each other.

The level of volunteerism in the community is remarkably high. Islanders have always helped their neighbours when they are in need. Food is taken to the elderly and sick when they find it difficult to look after themselves; money was raised for several low-income people who could not afford to buy their houses after the provincial settlement, and committees run the clubhouses. This working together is one indication of the community's strength.

One event illustrates this better than any mere description. In June of 1989 the Algonquin Island Association clubhouse burned to its foundations in a spectacular fire. Islanders were heartbroken, but out of the tears and sense of loss rose a determination to rebuild the AIA even better than before. Committees were set up to draw up plans and raise money. Once the design was fixed, crews of volunteer workers laboured all through that fall and winter. By New Year's Eve, Islanders celebrated with a huge dance in their unheated shell of a building. By the next spring the AIA building had been completed without any government subsidy.

The seasons play a larger role on the Islanders than they do in the city. Summer is the time to invite friends. There are long walks along the boardwalk, hanging out on the beach and meeting neighbours at the café. The intense competition of the Island Baseball League is gone now, but soccer has become an important sport. The summer dances at the WIA clubhouse are particularly special. The building is old now, but it has the same charming character as when it was built in 1938.

Gardens at 2 and 4 Nottawa Avenue, Algonquin Island

Islanders Deenie Anderson and Freda Lord, 1 Channel Avenue, Ward's Island

Gala Day is still celebrated on the August long weekend. Added on to that celebration is a new tradition of Island participation in the West Indian festival of Caribana. Shadowland, the Island Theatre Group, organizes this entry. For almost a month people work at "Mas Camp" preparing the costumes. Stilt-walking has become a speciality. On the Friday night of the Gala Weekend there is a fire parade, led by a rhythm band, through the community. Some of the people dress in their Caribana costumes, others are up on stilts, while many carry torches. At the end of the parade, there is a big bonfire on the beach with fire sculptures.

There is a saying that "you are only a true Islander after you have lived through the winter out on the sandbar." The coldest months have their own delights and hardships. The wind whipping across the bay can be so cold that a walk to the boat seems like a tundra outing, but the skating makes up for it. Every year the lagoons are frozen for six weeks or

Ward's Island Café

more and the bay is usually iced over for three or four weeks. Many Islanders are out on the ice every chance they can get. The iceboats are rigged and ready to go. Hockey games carry on for hours and skaters wander for miles across the expanse of the bay, sometimes pushed along with handheld sails.

Like any small community the Island has a closeness that is perhaps not possible in big city neighbourhoods, but it is not just its size that has drawn people together. Living

on an island has meant that people have learned to rely on one another for everything from a cup of sugar to help when there is an emergency. And the Island's history of struggle and collective effort has drawn people together in a special way. Friendships have been made in the process that will last a lifetime.

Few places in Canada have seen such continual change. There is little left of Elizabeth Simcoe's "favourite sands," except the sand itself. But one thing has remained constant

Island skaters at Algonquin lagoon

in the two hundred years since she walked on those sands: the Island has remained a unique place, strikingly different from the city.

It is not only that the Island looks different; there has always been a special sense about the people who have a connection with the place. Whether it was the fishermen of the early nineteenth century who struggled to make a life for themselves on the sand spit, or the cottagers in the heyday of Centre Island who loved that "sweet raffish"

place or the Islanders of today, all of them came to the Island to live a lifestyle of their own choosing. It is a place where difference and uniqueness and, yes, even oddity has been allowed and encouraged to thrive.

Toronto Island is a place that resonates with its history. It is not hard to imagine the Mississauga Indians spearing salmon in its lagoons. The results of one of the most important urban political struggles in the country can be seen in the vast park and remnants of the community. The

Janet Morton's bicycle art, 25 Third Street, Ward's Island

names are a testament to the Island's history. Blockhouse Bay, Gibraltar Point, Hanlan's Point, Ward's Island—each name has a story. Even the houses have their own history. Talk to any Islanders and they will tell you stories and legends about how the house they live in came to be built and who has lived there over the years.

If Toronto is a liveable city that works through the strength of its neighbourhoods, as many believe, then the Toronto Island community is its historic core, where the liveable city began and continues.

Garden art, 3 Seneca Avenue, Algonquin Island

SOURCES

Toronto Island has produced a rich crop of excellent books and articles that I have harvested to help produce this work.

The most outstanding work by far is Sally Gibson's book, *More than an Island*. It is rare that a community the size of Toronto Island has undergone such exhaustive treatment. Anyone wanting a detailed look at the Island and its history is urged to examine this book.

The other contemporary book that I enjoyed is Robert Sward's, *The Toronto Islands*. Sward does not attempt a comprehensive view of the Island, but he has a talent to tell interesting stories about fascinating events and people.

The most comprehensive collection of material on Toronto Island is in the Algonquin Island Archives, at 5 Ojibway Avenue, Toronto, M5J 2C9. The collection is the labour of love of Albert Fulton, archivist extraordinaire. The archives are open every Sunday from two to four p.m.

Over the years the Island and its many activities have been followed by journalists working for the daily press. These articles give a freshness and immediacy that is hard to capture decades later, and I have borrowed freely from this material. The best place to look for these articles is in the Metropolitan Toronto Reference Library.

The following is a short list of books on the Island:

Filey, Michael. *The Trillium and Toronto Island*. Toronto: Dundurn Publishing, 1976.

Gibson, Sally. *More than an Island*. Toronto: Irwin Publishing, 1984.

Lennon, M. J. *Memories of Toronto Island*. 1980.

Richmond, John. *A Tearful Tour of Toronto's Riviera of Yesterday*. Toronto: 1961.

Sward, Robert. *The Toronto Islands*.

Toronto Island Guide. Department of Agriculture, 1894.

Long pond, Centre Island

INDEX